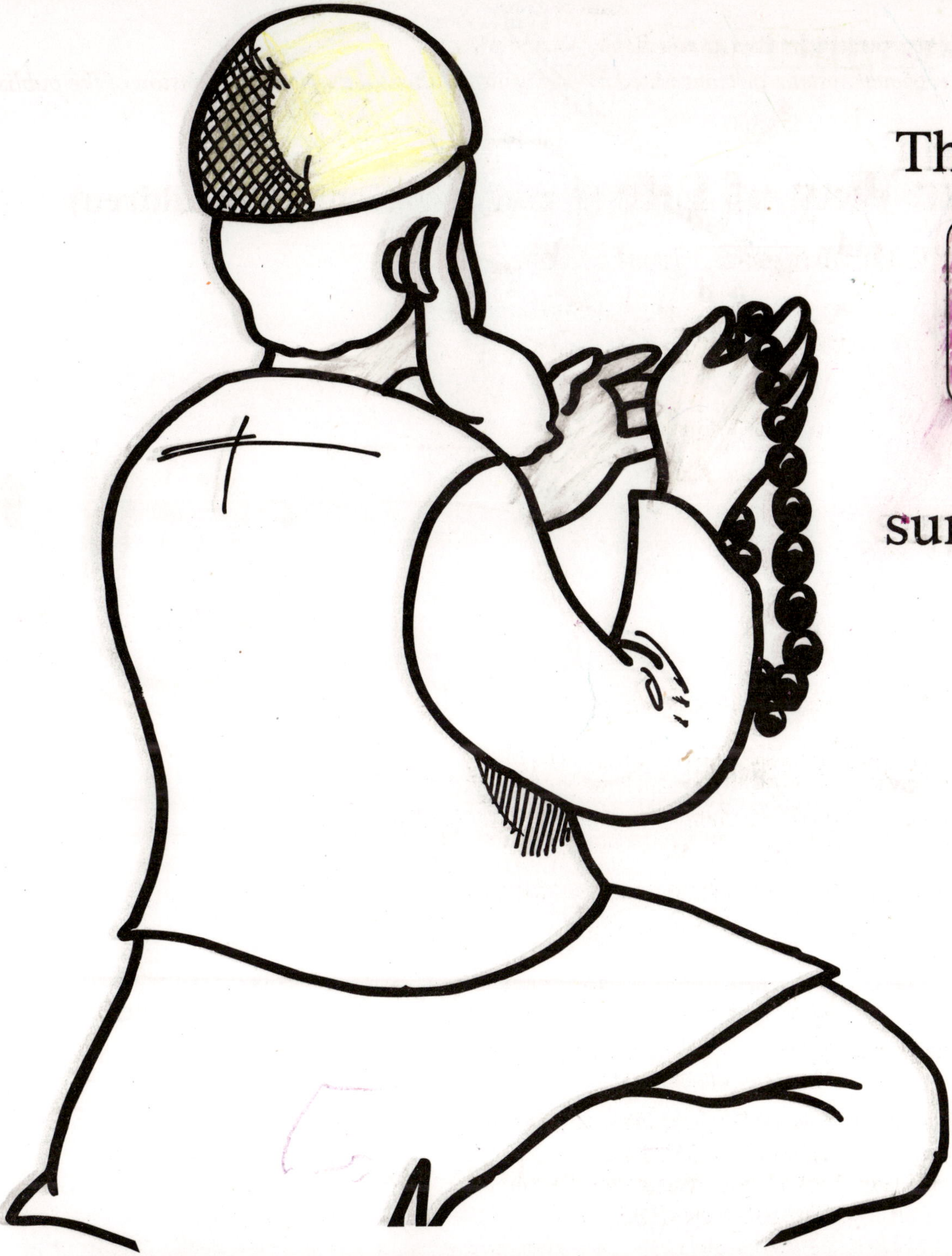

The name of our religion is

Islam

It means submission, surrender, obedience, peace and total faith.

The name of our Prophet is:

صلى الله عليه وسلم محمد رسول الله

Muhammad (S.A.W.)

He was the last and the Most Beloved Prophet of **Allah**

MUHAMMAD ﷺ was the LAST and The MOST BELOVED PROPHET of

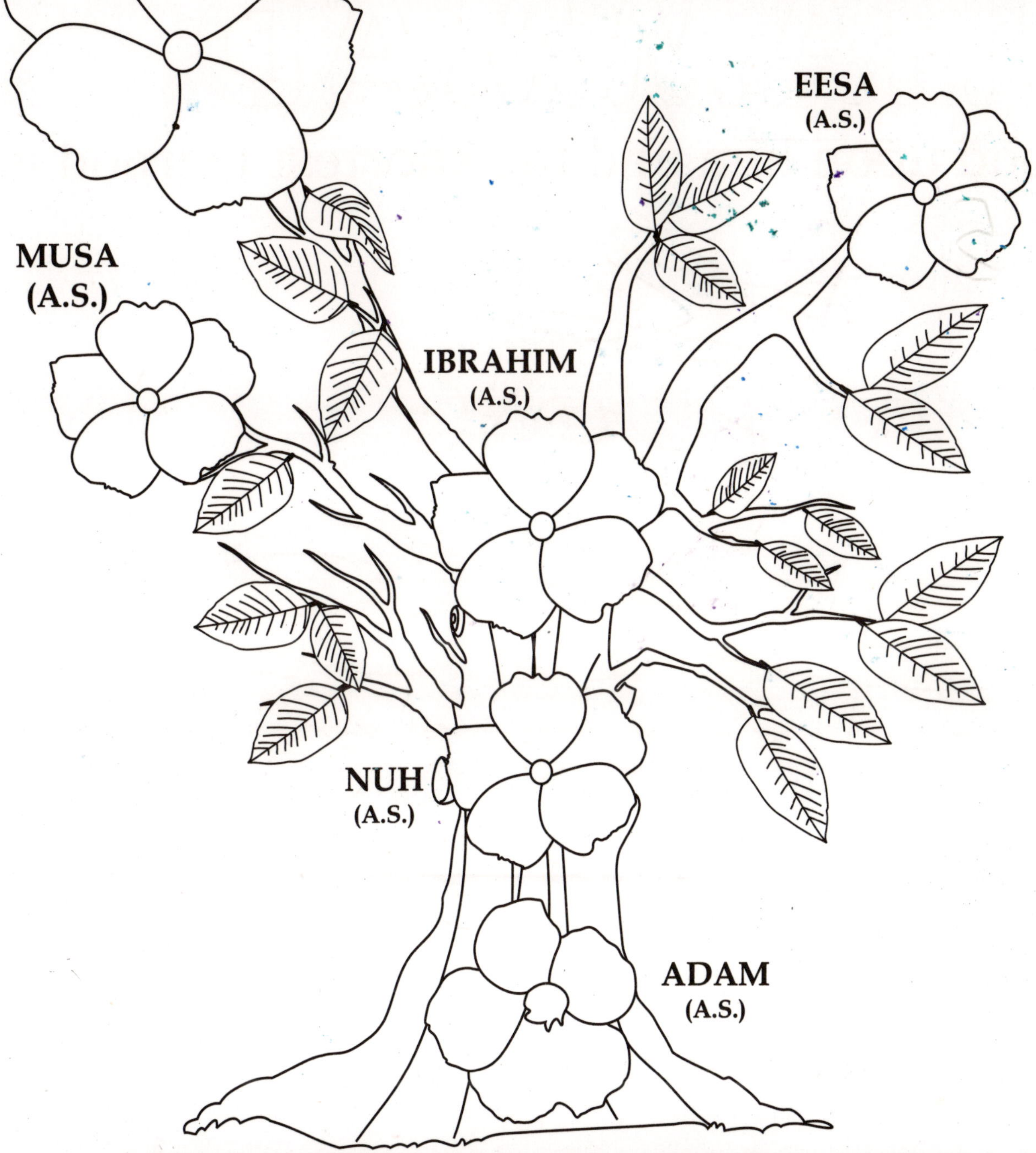

ALLAH

When we hear, read or say the Name of

MUHAMMAD

we must say: Durood upon him and the shortest Durood is:

صلى الله عليه وسلم

SALLALLAHU-ALAIHI-WASALLAM

The Prophet of Islam, Muhammad صلى الله عليه وسلم was born in Makkah

.... in Arabia.

MUHAMMAD

(Sallallahu-Alaihi-Wasallam)

was an honest and pious man. The entire nation called him.

Al-Amin

(The Truthful

and

Trustworthy)

His paternal grand father's name was Abd-ul Muttalib. and His maternal grand father's name was Wahb. His father's name was Abdullah and his mother's name was Aminah.

When his parents died, he began to live with his uncle Abu Talib who used to take him on business trips.

When he was young he married with a pious lady named Khadija.

KHADIJA

رضي الله عنها

Muhammad ﷺ had

SEVEN

Children

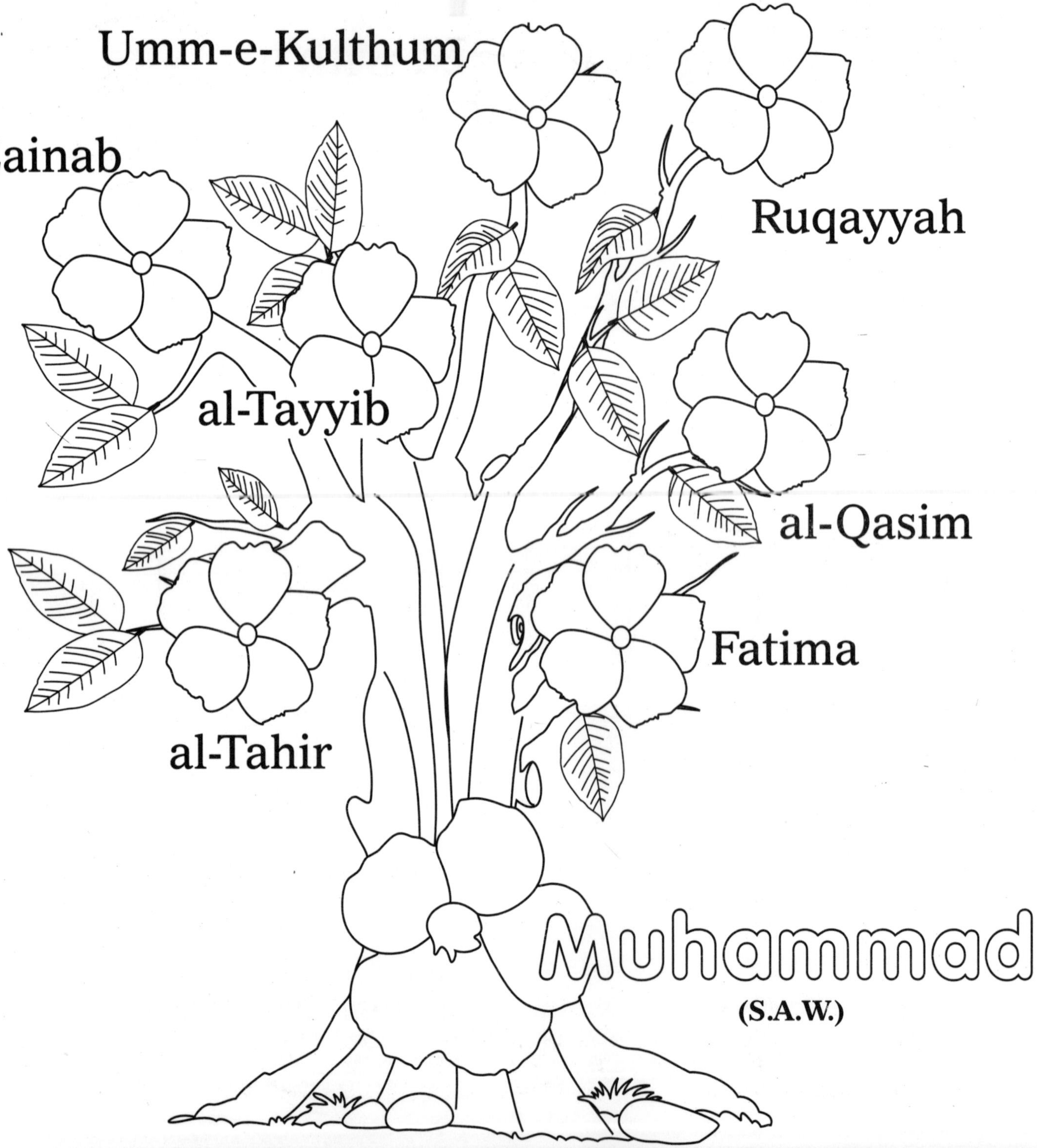

Muhammad (S.A.W.)

used to go to the cave of Hira

(Ghar-e-Hira),

in a mountain near Makkah spending time in seclusion and meditation.

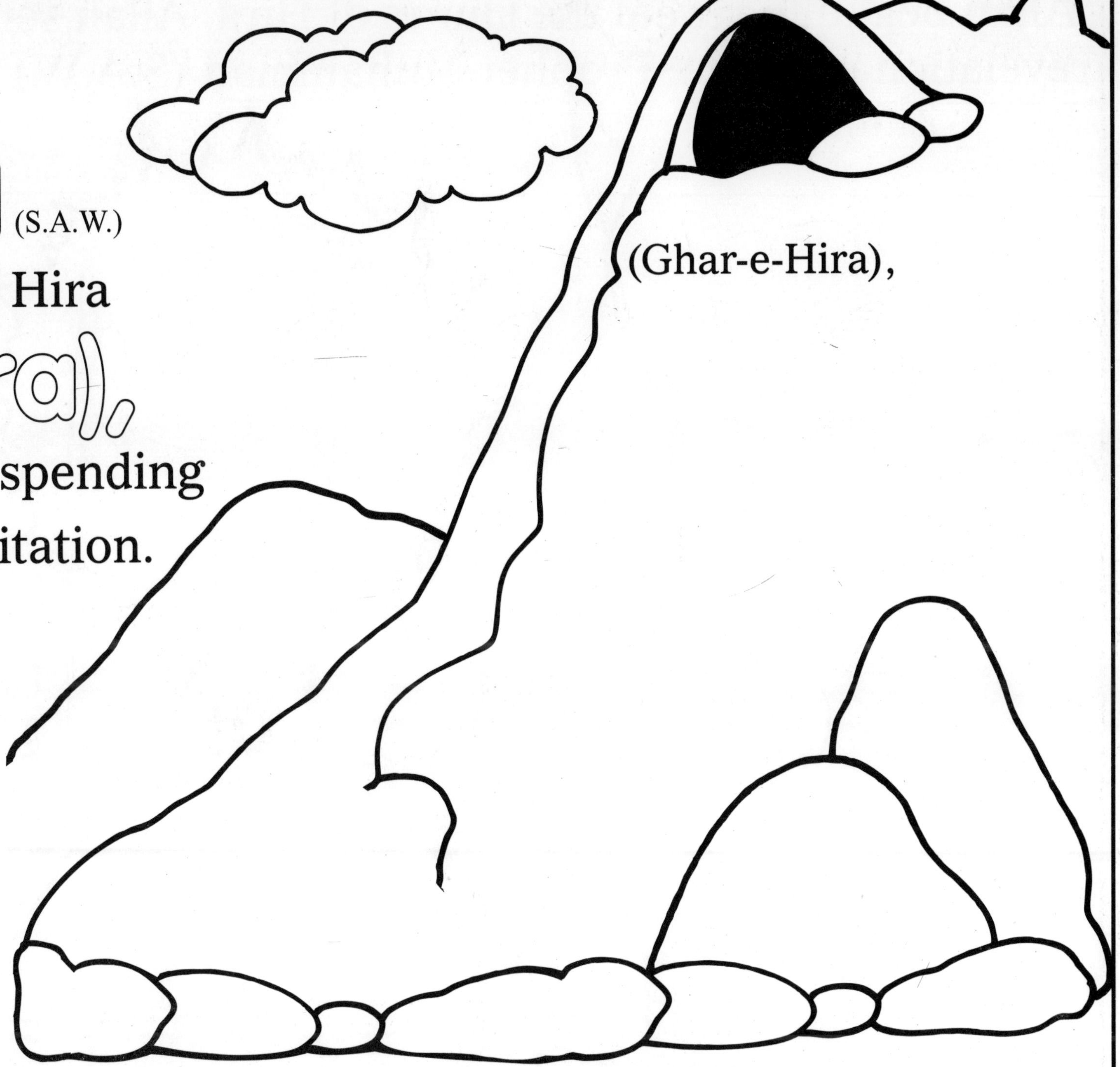

Allah began to reveal the Quran at Hira. Allah sent His Angel Gibrail (A.S.) for revelation upon the Prophet Muhammad (S.A.W.) the first words revealed were:

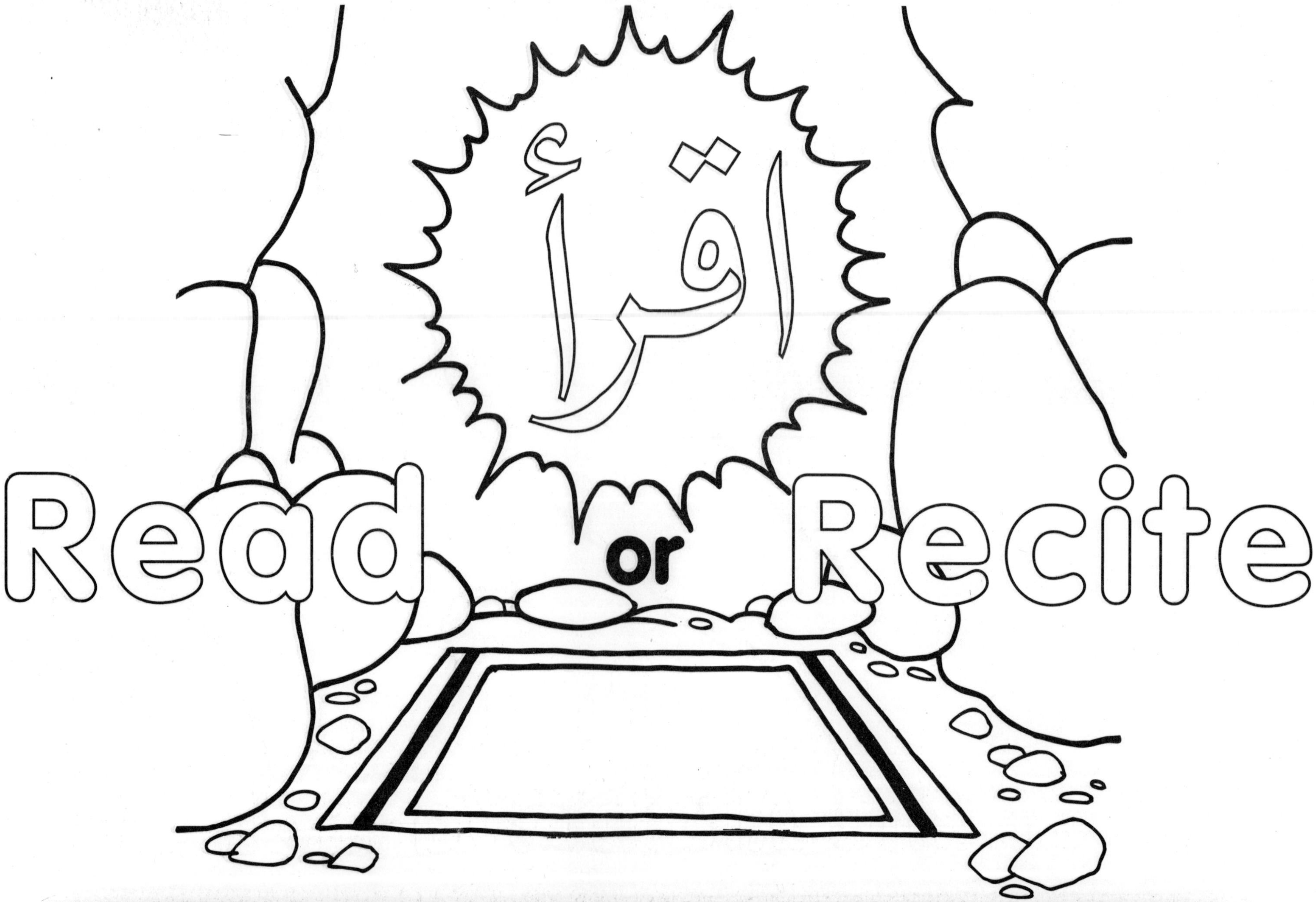

His heart was illuminated with the Divine Light making him the Messenger of Allah at the age of forty years. He began to preach the message of Allah. Now Muhammad (Sallallahu Alaihi Wa-Sallam) was Rusullah.

RASULULLAH

(The Prophet of Allah)

Muhammad

Sallallahu Alaihi Wa-Sallam

The disbelievers made much trouble for the believers. Rasulullah (ﷺ)and the believers were sent to a valley outside of Makkah to live for three years.

Allah told Muhammad (S.A.W.) and his Companions to make Hijra (Migration) to the city of

MADINA

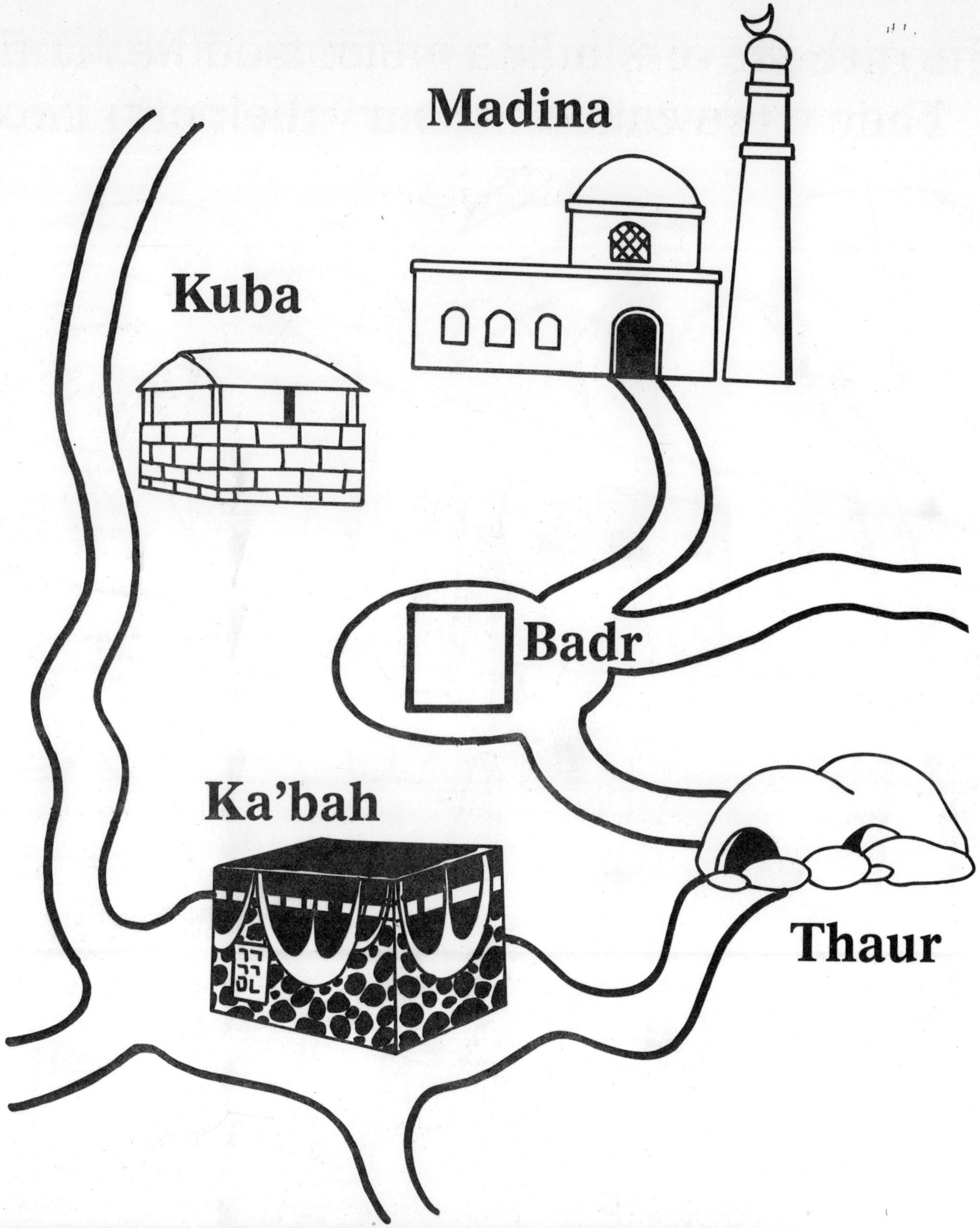

The people of Madina welcomed Muhammad (S.A.W.) and his Companions. They were called “Ansar” (helpers) because they helped the Muslims.

The year of Immigration of the Prophet (S.A.W.) and his companion to Madina, marks the beginning of the new Islamic Calendar which is called

HIJRI

Calendar

Islam is based on five pillars. First is

TAUHEED

(Al-Bukhari)

LA-ILAAHA IL-LAL-LAHU
MU-HAM-MA-DUR
RASULULLAH

Second pillar of Islam is

SALAH

(Al-Bukhari)

Third pillar of Islam is

SAWM

(Al-Bukhari)

Keep fast in the month of Ramadhan for purification of heart and mind. Recite the Holy Quran as much as you can in this month.

اَللّٰهُمَّ لَكَ صُمْتُ

وَبِكَ اٰمَنْتُ وَعَلٰى

رِزْقِكَ اَفْطَرْتُ

Fourth pillar of Islam is

ZAKAH

(Al-Bukhari)

Give poor-dues to the poor and the needy sincerely and regularly.

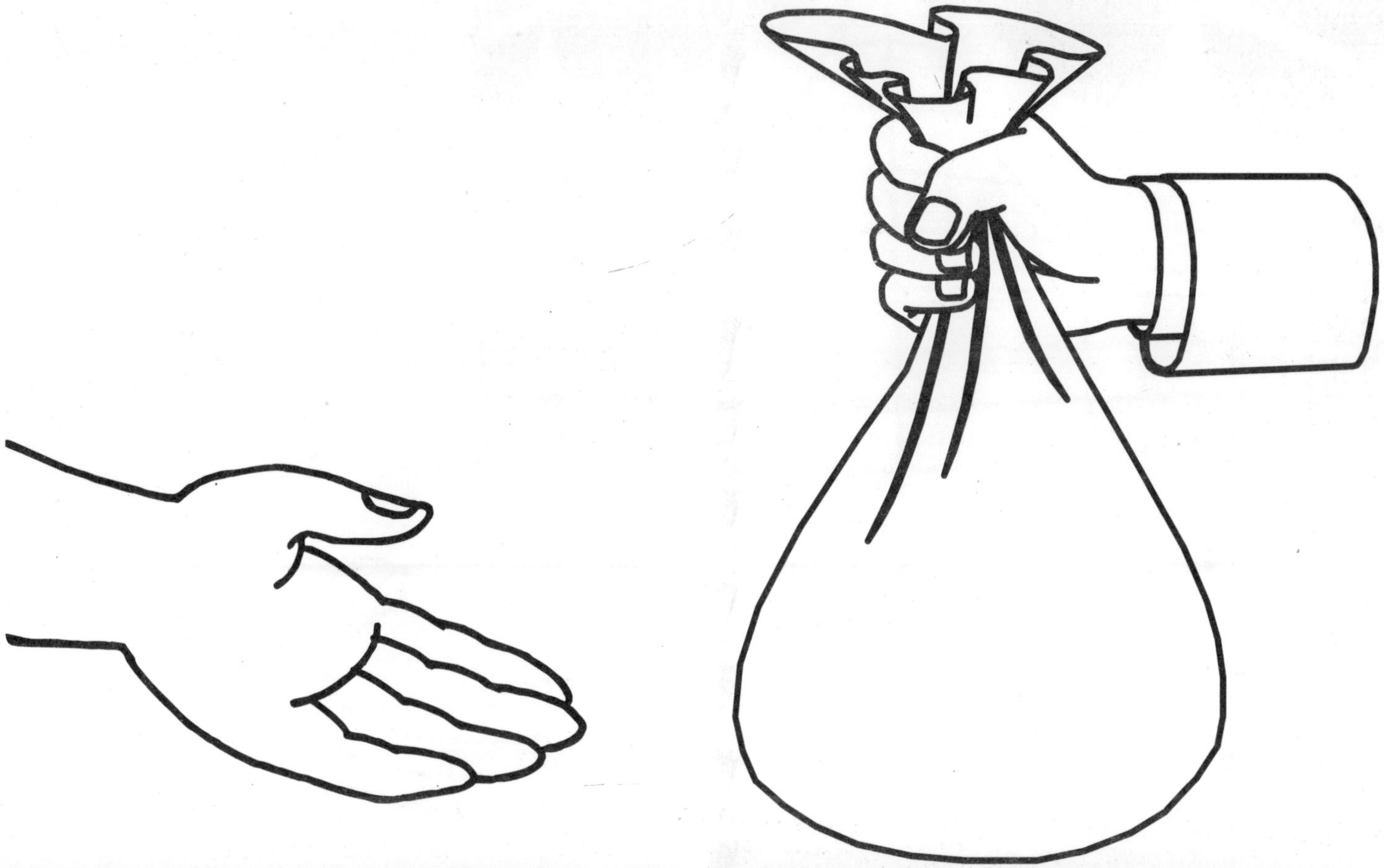

Fifth pillar of Islam is Pilgrimage to Ka'ba in Makkah in the month of Zil-Hajj when you are capable both financially and physically

(Al-Bukhari)

The Quran is the Holy Book of Islam, Recite the Quran with Tarteel and Tajweed as much as you can.

Whosoever follows a path to seek knowledge therein,
Allah will makeeasy for him a path to Paradise.

Rasulullah ﷺ told the Muslims: to greet each other with

Salaam (Peace be with you)

السلام عليكم

The sayings of Prophet Muhammad (S.A.W.) are called:

Allah is the Lord of the whole Universe. The entire universe with everything that it contains belongs to God Almighty. He alone is the creator, the nourisher, the sustainer and the real sovereign.

Allah

"Pay the labourer his wages before his sweat dries up."

(Ibn-e-Majah)

God loves those believers who labour to earn a living through lawful means.

If a Muslim clothes another of the faithful who is in dire need of clothing, he will be rewarded with apparel from Paradise by God on the Day of Judgement.

If a Muslim who serves water to another who is thirsty, will be rewarded with the water of the

Rivers of Paradise

(Al-Trimidhi)

If a Muslim, who feeds another who is hungry will be fed on the fruits of Paradise by God on the Day of Judgment

(Al-Trimidhi)

A Muslim should always speak the truth and should never utter a word of lie.

SPEAK THE
TRUTH

One who satiates himself, while his immediate neighbours go hungry is not a true believer.

(Ahmed Ibn Hanbal)

The best among you is he who learns the **Quran** and teaches it to others.

(Al-Bukhari)

Exchange gifts. "You will love each other."

(As-Sunan Al-Arb'a)

Allah will aid a slave (of His) so long as the slave aids his brother.

(Muslim)

لَا بَأْسَ طَهُوْرٌ إِنْ شَآءَ اللّٰهُ

لَا بَأْسَ طَهُوْرٌ إِنْ شَآءَ اللّٰهُ

اَللّٰهُمَّ اشْفِهِ اَللّٰهُمَّ عَافِهِ

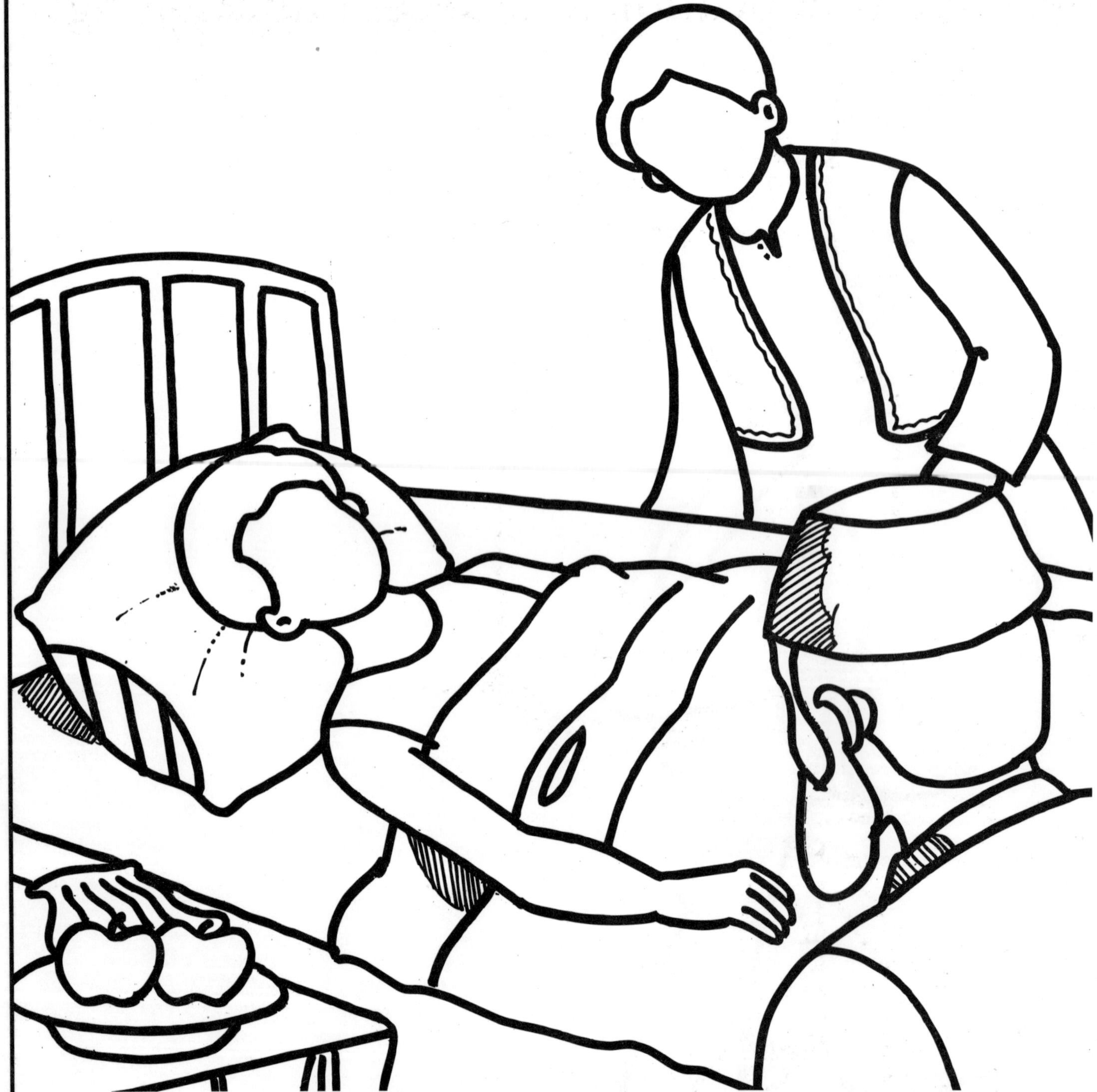

You should visit the sick,

(Al-Bukhari)

The best gift from a father to his child is education and decent upbringing.

(At-Tirmidhi)

Anyone who unjustly flogs his servant will be punished on the Day of Judgement

(At-Tabrani)

And every step you take to perform prayers is a charity.

Whosoever shields a Muslim, Allah will shield him in this world and the next.

(Muslim)

"Salah in Jama'ah is better than salah by one's self in one's house twenty-seven times."

(Al-Bukhari and Muslim)

“Cleanliness is half of one’s faith.”

(Muslim)

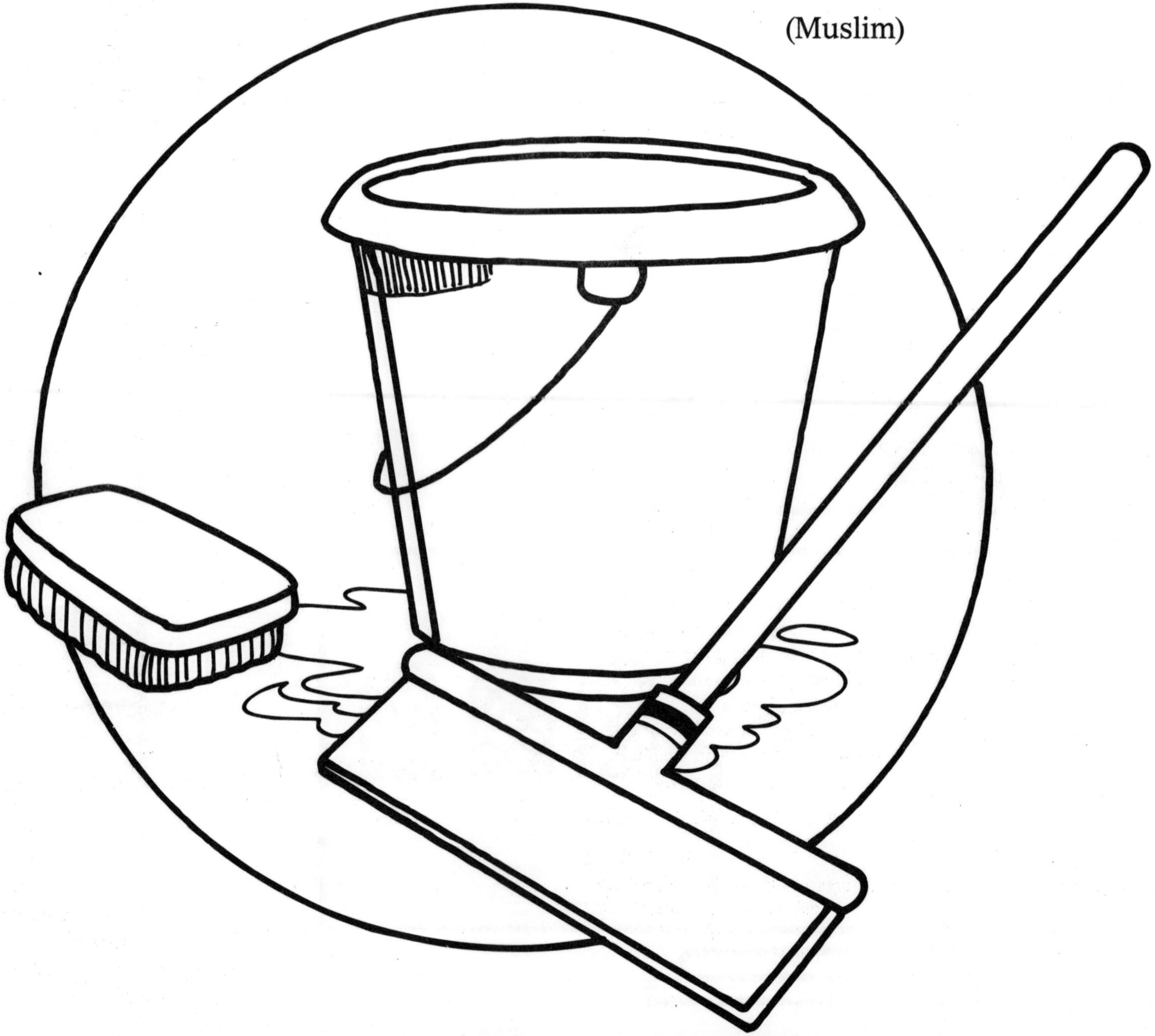

"Five things are the sunnat of the Ambiya Alaihis Salaam; Modesty, Tolerance, Cupping, using the Miswak and applying itr."

(**Muhammad** S.A.W.)

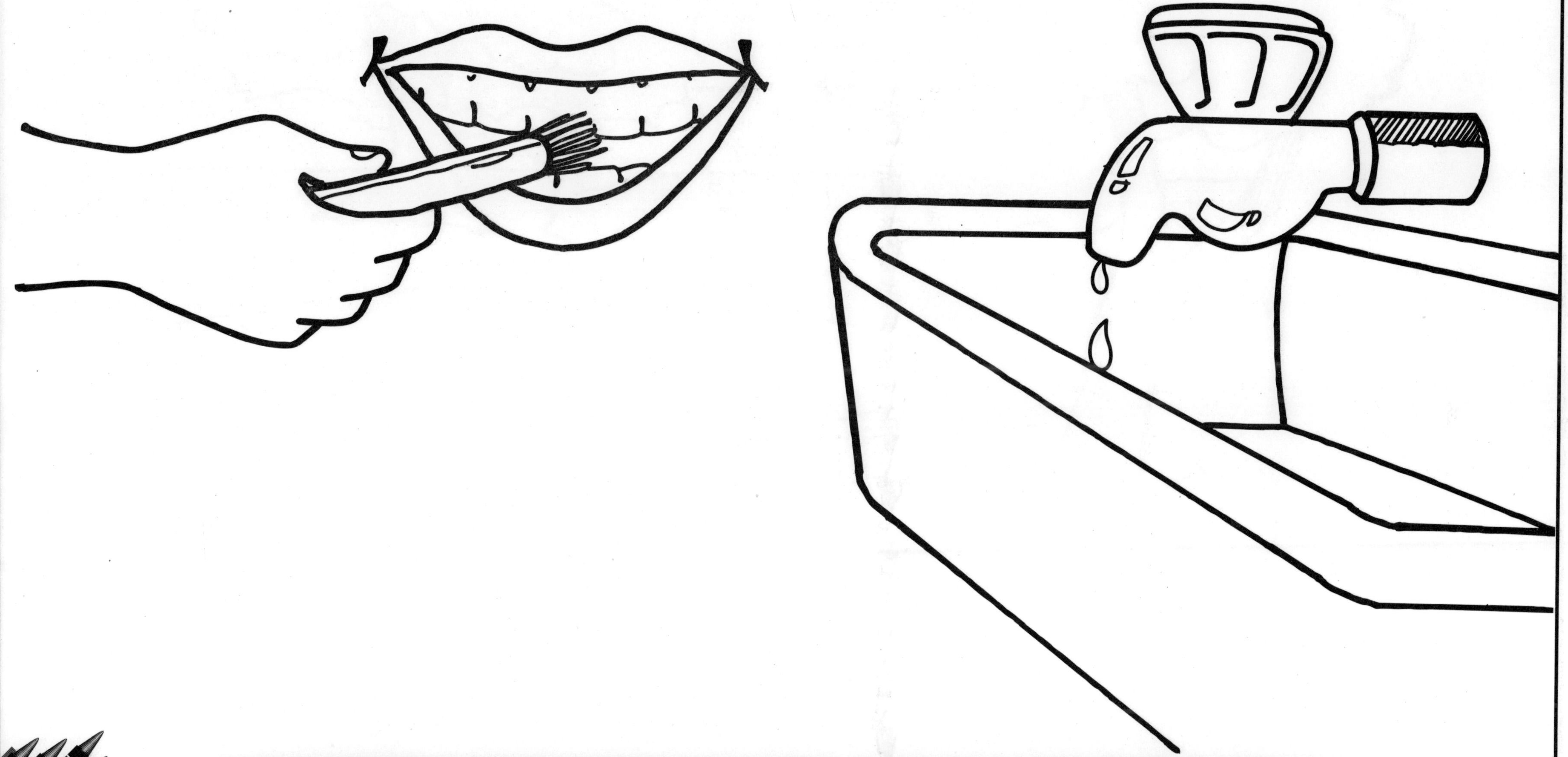

"You will not become true Muslims until you have love for each other."

(Muslim)

When a man plants a tree or cultivates a farm which provides food for birds, men and animals, the eating of it will be counted as charity for him.

(Ahmad, At-Tirmidhi)

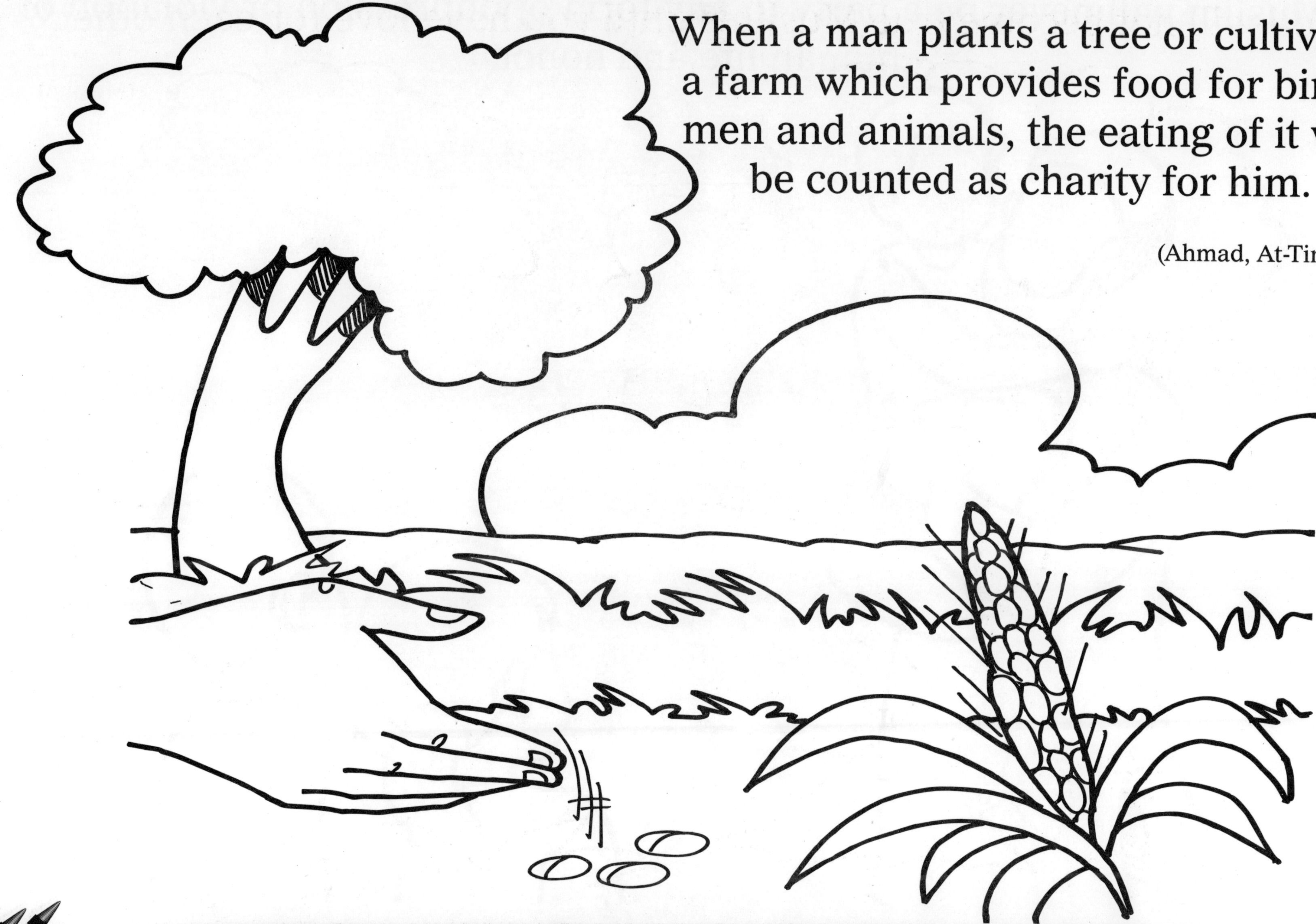

A Muslim will never be a party to any form of oppression or violation of human life and honor.

And removing a harmful thing from the road is a charity

Du'a offered by the Prophet at the time of going to bed.

اَللّٰهُمَّ بِاسْمِكَ اَمُوْتُ وَاَحْيٰى

In Thy name, O Allah: I shall die and in Thy,
name I shall live.

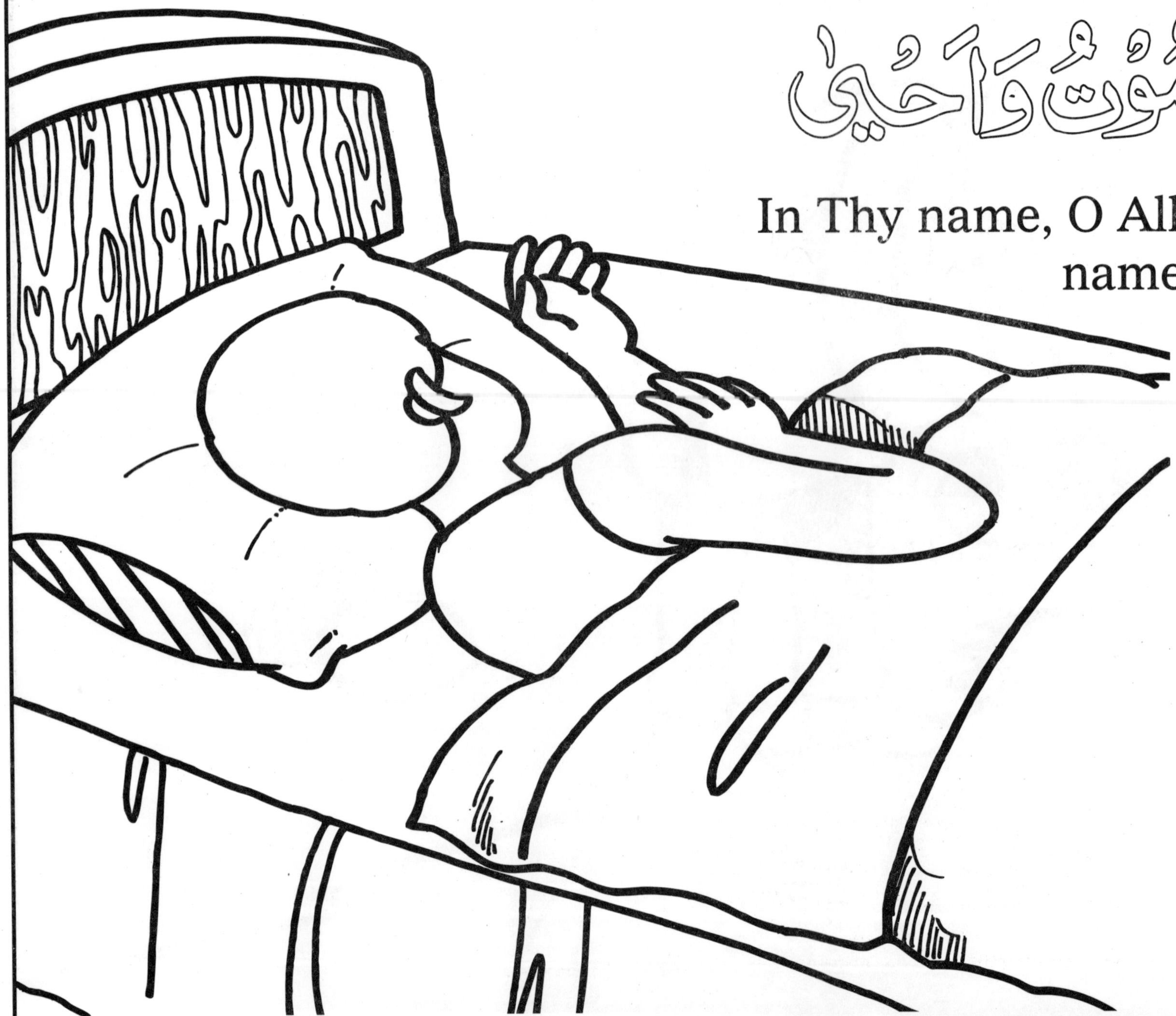

Du'a after eating.

الحمد لله الذي أطعمنا وسقانا
وجعلنا من المسلمين

Praise to be God who fed us, and gave us drink and made us Muslims.

Du'a at the time of entering the mosque.

اَللّٰهُمَّ افْتَحْ لِيْ
أَبْوَابَ رَحْمَتِكَ ط

O Allah! Open to me the doors of Thy mercy.

Du’a at the time of coming out of the mosque.

اَللّٰهُمَّ اِنِّيْٓ اَسْـَٔلُكَ

مِنْ فَضْلِكَ ط

I beg of Thee Thy bounty.

References for Ahadeeth mentioned in this book:

Page No.	Reference
17	AL- Bukhari
18	AL- Bukhari
19	AL- Bukhari
20	AL- Bukhari
21	AL- Bukhari
27	Ibn-e-Majah
30	At-Tirmidhi
31	At-Tirmidhi
33	Ahmed Ibn-e-Hambal
34	AL- Bukhari
35	As-Sunan Al-Arb'a
36	AL-Muslim
37	AL- Bukhari
38	At-Tirmidhi
39	At-Tabrani
41	AL-Muslim
42	AL- Bukhari and Muslim
43	AL-Muslim
44	Muhammad (Sallallahu Alaihi Wa-Sallam)
46	AL-Muslim
47	Ahmed, At-Tirmidhi